MW01264386

LET'S
see

The National Anthem

by Pamela Dell

Content Adviser: Kathryn V. Kingsbury,
Elementary school teacher, Hershey, Pennsylvania

Reading Adviser: Dr. Linda D. Labbo, Department of Reading Education,
College of Education, The University of Georgia

Let's See Library
Compass Point Books
Minneapolis, Minnesota

Compass Point Books
3109 West 50th Street, #115
Minneapolis, MN 55410

Visit Compass Point Books on the Internet at *www.compasspointbooks.com* or e-mail your
request to *custserv@compasspointbooks.com*

On the cover: Early sheet music of "The Star-Spangled Banner" and musical notes for the song

Photographs ©: Sam DeVincent Collection of Illustrated American Sheet Music, Archives Center, National
Museum of American History, Behring Center, Smithsonian Institution, cover; Reuters NewMedia Inc./Corbis,
4, 6, 20; Bettmann/Corbis, 8, 10, 14; Smithsonian Institution, National Museum of American History, © 2002,
12; Phil Schermeister/Corbis, 16; Corbis, 18.

Editor: Catherine Neitge
Photo Researcher: Marcie C. Spence
Designers/Page Production: Melissa Kes and Jaime Martens/Les Tranby

Library of Congress Cataloging-in-Publication Data
Dell, Pamela.
    The national anthem / by Pamela Dell.
        p. cm. — (Let's see)
Includes bibliographical references and index.
Contents: What is an anthem?—What is the American national anthem?—Who wrote "The Star-Spangled
Banner"?—What is a star-spangled banner? Why was "The Star-Spangled Banner" written?—Who made the
star-spangled banner that Francis Scott Key wrote about?—Who wrote the music to "The Star-Spangled
Banner"?—When did "The Star-Spangled Banner" become the national anthem?—When is the American
national anthem played?
ISBN 0-7565-0619-0
1. Baltimore, Battle of, Baltimore, Md., 1814—Juvenile literature. 2. Star-spangled banner (Song)—Juvenile
literature. 3. Key, Francis Scott, 1779-1843—Juvenile literature. 4. United States—History—War of 1812—
Flags—Juvenile literature. 5. Flags—United States—History—19th century—Juvenile literature. [1. Baltimore,
Battle of, Baltimore, Md., 1814. 2. Star-spangled banner (Song) 3. Key, Francis Scott, 1779-1843. 4. United
States—History—War of 1812. 5. Flags—United States.] I. Title. II. Series.
    E356.B2D45 2004
    782.42'1599'0973—dc21   2003014459

Table of Contents

NOTE: In this book, words that are defined in the glossary
are in **bold** the first time they appear in the text.

What Is an Anthem?

People all over the world sing songs about their countries. An anthem is a song that praises a country. Sometimes anthems are also written to praise God or a saint. Some anthems are like prayers. Others are loud, joyful songs of pride.

Most countries have one important anthem that all the people know. It is a song that has special meaning to the citizens of that country. The people feel proud of their country when they sing this anthem. They feel loyal when they hear the music being played. This special song of praise is called a national anthem.

◄ Students from a French-American school in Boston sing the national anthems of France and the United States as they stand near each country's flag.

What Is the National Anthem of the United States?

The national anthem of the United States is called "The Star-Spangled Banner." It has four verses. Usually only the first verse is sung. The words to the first verse are:

Oh, say can you see by the dawn's early light

*What so proudly we hailed at the twilight's last **gleaming?***

*Whose broad stripes and bright stars through the **perilous** fight,*

*O'er the **ramparts** we watched were so **gallantly** streaming?*

And the rocket's red glare, the bombs bursting in air,

Gave proof through the night that our flag was still there.

Oh, say does that star-spangled banner yet wave

O'er the land of the free and the home of the brave?

◀ *Cincinnati Reds fans wave American flags during the singing of the national anthem before the start of a baseball game.*

Who Wrote the National Anthem?

Francis Scott Key wrote a poem that became "The Star-Spangled Banner." He was on a boat in the waters near Baltimore, Maryland, on September 13, 1814. The British were bombing Fort McHenry and trying to capture the city of Baltimore. Key had been stopped by British soldiers.

Key had strong feelings for his country. As he waited out the battle, he worried. Would his country's soldiers win this fight? Key wrote his famous poem after the battle ended. It began as a few words on the back of a letter. It was the only thing he had to write on. The next day, he wrote his words on paper and added more verses.

◀ Francis Scott Key watched the bombing of Fort McHenry from aboard ship.

Why Was "The Star-Spangled Banner" Written?

The battle near Baltimore was part of the War of 1812. The war was between the United States and Great Britain. Key was in Baltimore to do a special job. The British were holding an important American prisoner on one of their ships. Key was a 35-year-old lawyer from Washington, D.C. He had been sent to get the prisoner. The British soldiers made him wait until the fight for Baltimore was over.

Key waited all night to see what would happen. Finally, dawn came. Through the smoke, Key saw a wonderful sight. It was the American flag still flying over Fort McHenry. It proved the Americans had won!

◄ *Francis Scott Key saw the American flag still flying after the battle.*

What Is a Star-Spangled Banner?

A flag is sometimes called a banner. A spangle is something small that shines. It also means a sparkly decoration. Francis Scott Key saw the shining white stars on the American flag as spangles. His words "star-spangled banner" meant the American flag.

Key's poem was about one special flag. That flag had eight red stripes and seven white stripes. It was spangled with 15 stars. Today, the American flag has seven red stripes and six white stripes. It is spangled with 50 stars. Each star stands for a state.

◀ *The original flag that inspired Francis Scott Key's famous poem*

Who Made the Flag for Fort McHenry?

Major George Armistead was the commander of Fort McHenry during the War of 1812. He wanted a giant American flag for the fort. He wanted to make sure the British would see it easily from far away.

Armistead hired a skilled flag maker to sew the flag for Fort McHenry. Her name was Mary Young Pickersgill. Her daughter Caroline helped her make the flag.

The finished flag was huge. It was 30 feet by 42 feet (9 meters by 13 meters). Each of the 15 stripes was 2 feet wide (61 centimeters). Each star measured 26 inches (66 cm) from point to point.

◀ *The original flag was moved from Fort McHenry to Boston Navy Yard for display in 1874.*

Who Wrote the Music?

Francis Scott Key did not write the music to his famous song. He wrote the words in the form of a poem. Many copies of the poem were printed on **handbills** for others to read. The handbills included a note that said: *Tune: "To Anacreon in Heaven."* This was the title of a song about the ancient Greek poet Anacreon. It was the tune that Key chose to go with his words. Soon, his poem became known everywhere as "The Star-Spangled Banner."

"To Anacreon in Heaven" was a popular English song. An English **composer** named John Stafford Smith probably wrote the music to this song.

◄ *Two high school saxophonists practice "The Star-Spangled Banner" before a parade.*

When Did It Become the National Anthem?

"The Star-Spangled Banner" grew more and more popular during the 1800s. During the Civil War (1861–1865), both Northern and Southern troops sang the song.

It became the unofficial anthem of the Army and the Navy, which played the song during important ceremonies. It was not until March 3, 1931, however, that "The Star-Spangled Banner" became the most important song for the whole country. That day, President Herbert Hoover signed a law that made it the official national anthem.

◄ President Herbert Hoover made the national anthem official in 1931.

When Is the National Anthem Played?

The Navy was the first to play "The Star-Spangled Banner" during flag-raising ceremonies. It began doing this in 1889. Now, this is a common practice. The national anthem is always played at important events for the nation.

It is played when a new president of the United States takes office. Someone famous always sings the national anthem before big sports events begin. When an American wins a medal at the Olympic Games, "The Star-Spangled Banner" is played.

For nearly two centuries, the words of "The Star-Spangled Banner" have brought pride to the people of "the land of the free and the home of the brave."

◀ *Baltimore Orioles players stand for the national anthem before a baseball game. A replica of the original star-spangled banner hangs over the wall behind center field.*

Glossary

composer—one who writes music
gallantly—not afraid in battle; proudly or fearlessly
gleaming—shining or glowing
handbills—single pieces of paper with messages on them, like fliers

perilous—dangerous
ramparts—walls or some other form of sturdy protection

Did You Know?

• At first, Francis Scott Key named his song, "In Defence of Fort M'Henry."

• "The Star-Spangled Banner" first appeared in a newspaper on September 20, 1814. The newspaper was the Baltimore Patriot. The first time both music and words were performed together was in Baltimore on October 19, 1814.

• The original handmade flag has just undergone a long restoration project. Experts at the Smithsonian's National Museum of American History in Washington, D.C., have been working on the flag for several years.

• Part of the Fort McHenry star-spangled banner is now missing. Pieces of it were given to the fort's soldiers or their wives. Today, the flag measures 30 feet by 34 feet (9 m by 10.4 m).

• Francis Scott Key was born at Terra Rubra Farm in Keymar, Maryland. An American flag was raised there on May 30, 1949. It has never been taken down since.

• The Maryland Historical Society bought Key's first handwritten copy of "The Star-Spangled Banner" in 1953. The society paid $26,400 for it.

Want to Know More?

In the Library

Bowdish, Lynea, and Harry Burman. *Francis Scott Key and The Star-Spangled Banner.* New York: Mondo Publishing, 2002.

Kroll, Steven. *By the Dawn's Early Light: The Story of the Star-Spangled Banner.* New York: Scholastic Trade, 2000.

Quiri, Patricia Ryon. *The National Anthem.* New York: Children's Press, 1998.

On the Web

For more information on the *national anthem,* use FactHound to track down Web sites related to this book.

1. Go to *www.compasspointbooks. com/facthound*
2. Type in this book ID: 0756506190
3. Click on the *Fetch It* button.

Your trusty FactHound will fetch the best Web sites for you!

Through the Mail

Fort McHenry National Monument and Historic Shrine
2400 E. Fort Ave.
Baltimore, MD 21230
410/962-4290
For information about Fort McHenry, its famous flag, and the War of 1812

On the Road

National Museum of American History
14th Street and Constitution Avenue N.W.
Washington, DC 20560
202/357-2700
To see the original star-spangled banner that inspired Francis Scott Key

The Star-Spangled Banner Flag House and War of 1812 Museum
844 E. Pratt St.
Baltimore, MD 21202
410/837-1793
To see the original 1793 home of Mary Young Pickersgill and her daughter Caroline; one of the oldest museums in Baltimore

Index

About the Author
Pamela Dell was born in Idaho, grew up in Chicago, and now lives in Southern California. She began her professional career writing for adults and started writing for children about 12 years ago. Since then she has published fiction and nonfiction books, written numerous magazine articles, and created award-winning interactive multimedia. Among many other things, Pamela loves technology, the Internet, books, movies, curious people, and cats, especially black cats.